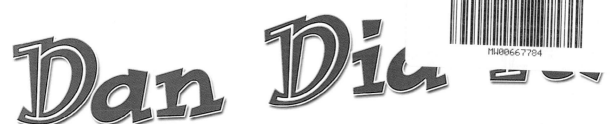

Dan Did It

By D.M. Longo

Illustrated by Tony Sansevero

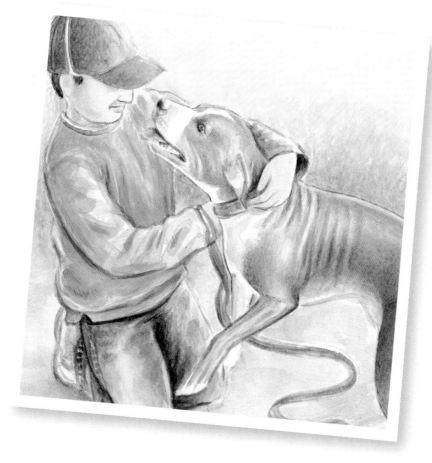

Target Skill Consonants Dd/d/ and Kk/k/

PEARSON

Scott Foresman

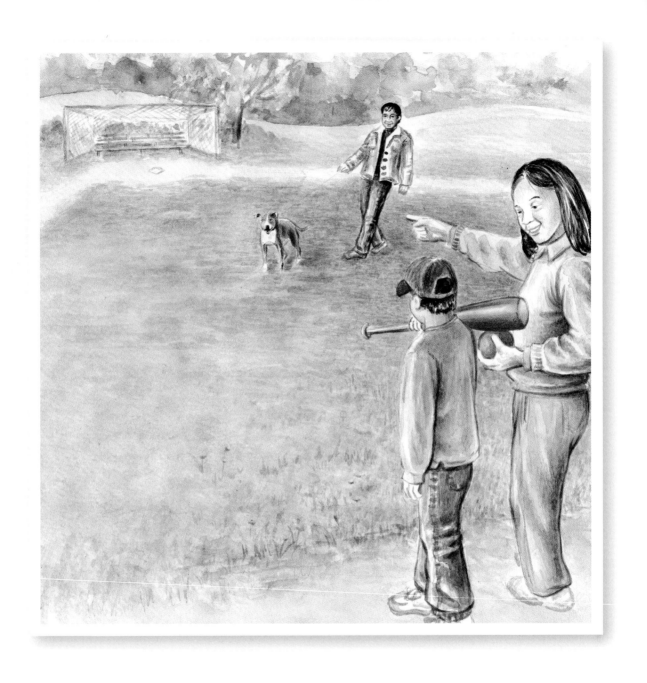

Can Dan see it?

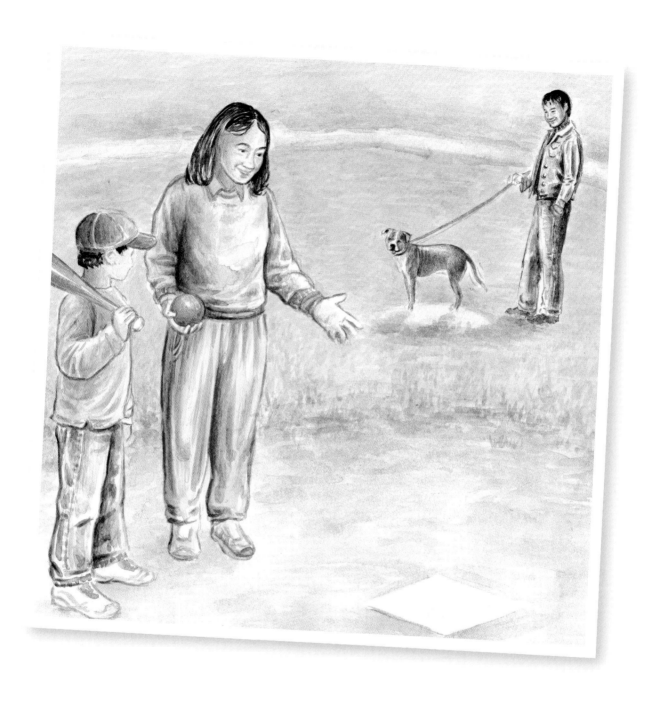

Dan, look at it!

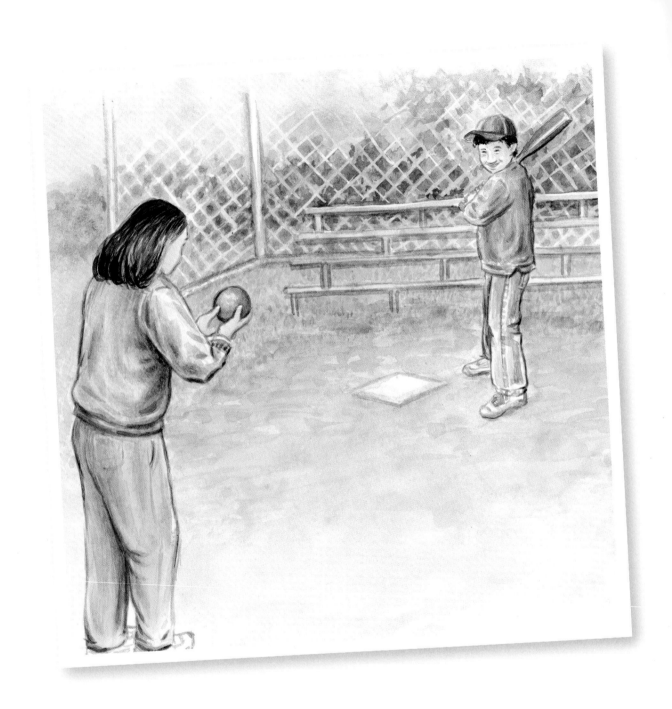

Can Dan hit it?

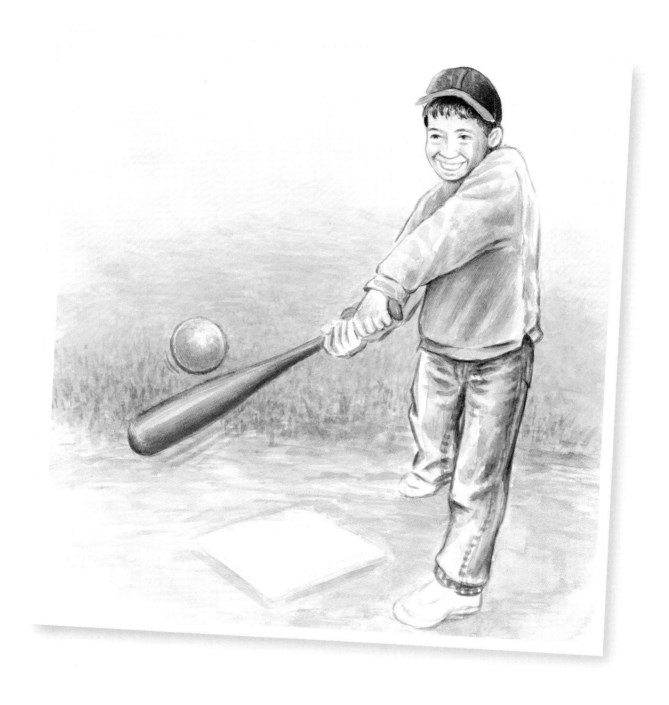

Look! Dan did it!

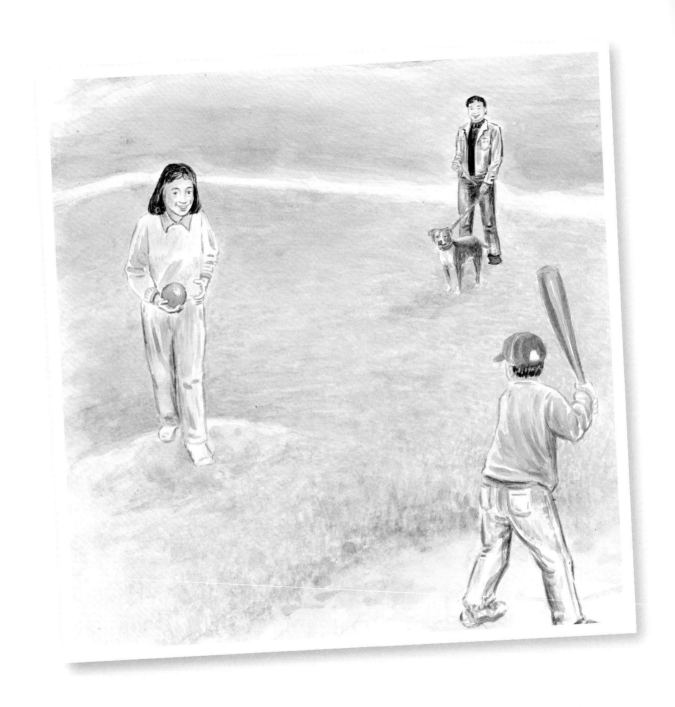

Can Dan see Kip?

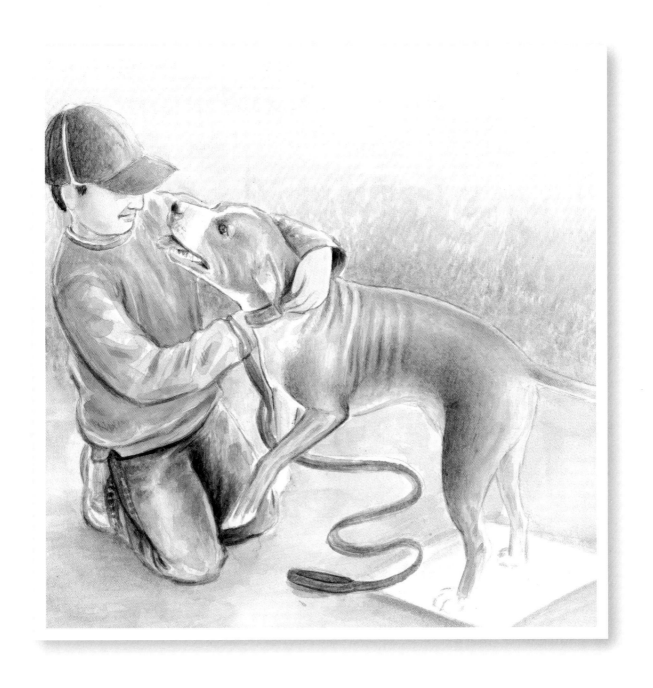

Look at Kip, Dan!

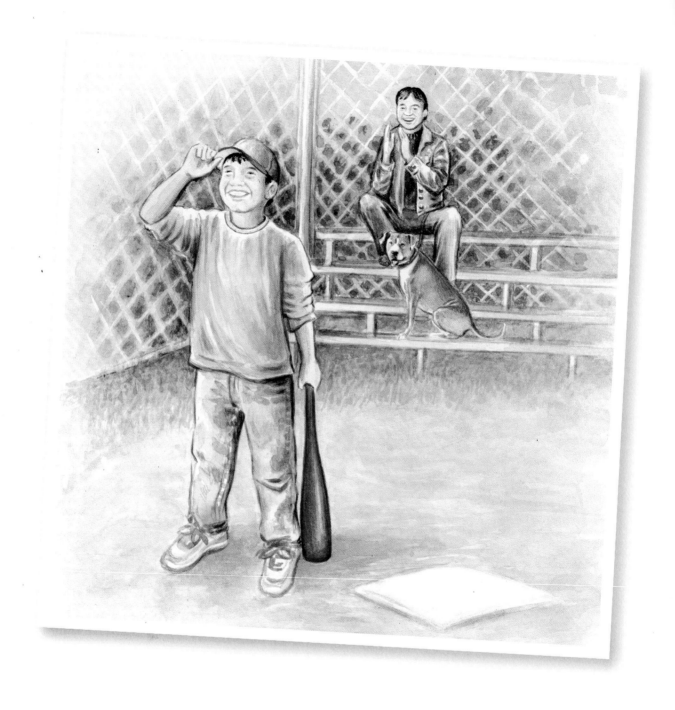

See! Dan did it!